THE promise OF HOPE

EMILIE BARNES

Paintings by

Simon Bull

H HARVEST HOUSE PUBLISHERS

EUGENE, OREGON

THE promise OF HOPE

Text Copyright © 2002 by Emilie Barnes
Published by Harvest House Publishers
Eugene, Oregon 97402

ISBN 0-7369-0894-3

For more information about other books and products available
from Emilie Barnes, please send a self-addressed, stamped envelope to:

More Hours in My Day
2150 Whitestone Drive
Riverside, CA 92506
(909) 369-4093

All works of art reproduced in this book are copyrighted by Simon Bull
and may not be copied or reproduced without the artist's permission.
For more information regarding Simon Bull art prints, please contact:

Media Arts Group, Inc.
900 Lightpost Way
Morgan Hill, CA 95037
1.800.366.3733

Text from this book previously appeared in *A Cup of Hope*
by Emilie Barnes (Harvest House Publishers, 2000) and
Help Me Trust You, Lord by Emilie Barnes (Harvest House Publishers, 1998).

Design & production by Koechel Peterson & Associates, Minneapolis, MN

Harvest House Publishers has made every effort to trace the ownership of all poems and quotes.
In the event of a question arising from the use of a poem or quote, we regret any error made
and will be pleased to make the necessary correction in future editions of this book.

Unless otherwise indicated, Scripture quotations are taken from the Holy Bible,
New International Version®, Copyright © 1973, 1978, 1984 by the International Bible Society.
Used by permission of Zondervan Publishing House.

Printed in Hong Kong

02 03 04 05 06 07 08 09 10 11 /NG / 10 9 8 7 6 5 4 3 2 1

without
HOPE,
Life
as we know it
is simply

impossible

The Promise of Hope

THE HOPE THAT RESIDES DEEP INSIDE you is stronger than you think. It's a survival mechanism built into you by the Master Designer. Even when it seems to be ebbing low, if you'll give it a chance, it will probably bubble back up again.

Whether the rain in your own life is a steady, wearying drizzle, a dramatic deluge, or just a threatening cloud on the horizon, I want you to know that God's purpose in it all is to draw you closer into his warm embrace and then use you to draw others to him as well.

I was just thinking one morning during meditation how much alike hope and baking powder are: quietly getting what is best in me to rise, awakening the hint of eternity within.

MARCINA WIEDERKEHR

Hope is a feeling. It's a sense of buoyant optimism, a sense that everything's going to be all right in the time to come. A feeling of hope is what puts a spring in your step as you step toward the future. It gives you energy and momentum, and makes you want to accomplish a lot. It's a wonderful thing to feel hopeful. We need that shot of energy that comes with hopeful emotions.

Trust in the Lord and do good;
dwell in the land and enjoy safe pasture.
Delight yourself in the Lord
and he will give you the
desires of your heart.
Commit your way to the Lord;
trust in him and he will do this.

PSALM 37:3-5

And now, when the clouds seem to be lifting and the colors begin to shine through the clouds (but who knows what will happen in the future?), I can see so much more clearly the ways in which I have indeed been restored, supported, strengthened, and established. It didn't happen exactly the way I thought it would, but the results were so much deeper and more wonderful than I could imagine…But you and I could never know the wonderful things that God has in store for us when we bring him our overflowing cup of trouble…and then let him fill us to overflowing with his love.

healing

I HAVE COME TO BELIEVE there is a hope that lives deep within the human soul—deeper than feelings, deeper than thought.

Here on earth, the restoration we experience is an ongoing process, truly miraculous but partial and problematic. Here on earth, the very process of healing leaves us inevitably marked and scarred (not to mention wrinkled and sagging).

I have told you these things, so that in me you may have peace. In this world you will have trouble. But take heart! I have overcome the world.

JOHN 16:33

If seeds in the black earth can turn into such beautiful
roses, what might not the heart of man become in
its long journey toward the stars?

G. K. CHESTERTON

Nothing that is worth doing can be achieved in our lifetime; therefore we must be saved by hope. Nothing that is true or beautiful makes complete sense in any immediate context of history; therefore we must be saved by faith. Nothing we do, however virtuous, can be accomplished alone; therefore we must be saved by love. No virtuous act is quite as virtuous from the standpoint of our friend or foe as it is from our standpoint. There, we must be saved by the final form of love which is forgiveness.

REINHOLD NIEBUHR

GOD IS DOING A STRENGTHENING, healing, miraculous work in our lives.

His divine power has given us everything
we need for life and godliness
through our knowledge of him who
called us by his own glory and goodness.
Through these he has given us his very
great and precious promises, so that
through them you may participate
in the divine nature.

2 PETER 1:3-4

We can so easily get in a rut. Our world can become

humdrum. But let's dare to hope, to look forward

to something, and let's don't feel guilty about it.

It's a human need. Jesus told us not to be "anxious"

about the future. I don't think he told us not

to think about it or look forward to it. After all, he said

he came to bring us the abundant life. Isn't that worth

getting excited about and looking forward to?

BILL KINNAIRD

faith

FAITH ALWAYS TRAVELS hand in hand with hope—it's what enables us to keep our hopes up when the way becomes rockier and more obscure. Faith is what we need to keep moving on, moving up, trusting our Guide, trusting it will all be worth it.

But I will sing of your strength,
in the morning I will sing of your
love; for you are my fortress,
my refuge in times of trouble.
O my Strength, I sing praise to you;
you, O God, are my fortress,
my loving God.

PSALM 59:16-17

GOD HAS PROMISED to give me a future and a hope. If I trust his Word, the gifts he has in store for me will be unimaginably wonderful. There will be comfort and stability and dancing and feasting.

The cup of my life is still an earthen vessel, prone to leaks, sometimes overfull with bitterness and doubt and fear and resentment, still in need of being emptied and then refilled by God.

But now, somehow, it feels like a deeper cup, a stronger cup. And when I persist in surrendering it to my heavenly Father, it seems to bubble and brim and overflow with more and more of the Lord's goodness.

ACCEPT YOUR GOOD DAYS as they're given—as gifts of hope, as glimpses of heaven while we're still on earth, as reminders that even the best days of our lives are simply little tastes of the timeless joy that God has in store for us as we draw ever closer to him.

I can't keep myself from failing in sometimes minor, sometimes spectacular ways. And the deeper that realization becomes, the more vital it becomes that I learn to turn it all over to the one who really is in control of the past, the present, and the future.

My heavenly Father is the one who truly knows the end from the beginning. He and only he can fill my cup to overflowing with good things.

HOPE REQUIRES STRENGTH—sometimes all the strength you can muster. But hope also gives you strength. Hope energizes. Hope moves you forward. When you dare to hope, you can do so much more than you ever thought.

And yes, hope requires courage—but hoping can make you brave. It makes the sacrifices seem worthwhile.

And hope certainly requires endurance. But hope helps you endure. Hope will carry you further through suffering and trials than almost any quality. For hope is often the thing that kicks in to endure when physical, emotional, and mental strength is gone. It's one of those seemingly fragile qualities that endure when more robust attitudes have failed.

Do not look forward to the changes and chances of this life in fear; rather look to them with the full hope that, as they arise, God, whose you are, will deliver you out of them. He has kept you hitherto—do you but hold fast to his dear hand, and he will lead you safely through all things; and, when you cannot stand, he will bear you in his arms. Do not look forward to what may happen tomorrow; the same everlasting Father who cares for you today will take care of you tomorrow, and every day. Either he will shield you from suffering, or he will give you unfailing strength to bear it. Be at peace, then, and put aside all anxious thoughts and imaginations.

FRANCIS DE SALES

strength

I CAN LEAN ON THE strength of my Lord God, who has promised to be strongest when I am weak. Again and again, that promise has proved to be true. In so many areas of my life, I am finding, I really can't do it all myself. But God can. And maybe that's the whole point.

There is nothing I can do to keep my cup from overflowing with trouble. Except one thing. There is one thing that I, and you, and anyone who is facing trouble can do and must do, again and again. We can carry that overflowing cup, messy and sloppy as it is, to the foot of the cross and leave it there.

A cup that is already full cannot have more added to it. In order to receive the further good to which we are entitled, we must give of that which we have.

MARGARET BECKER

Consider it pure joy, my brothers, whenever you face trials of many kinds, because you know that the testing of your faith develops perseverance. Perseverance must finish its work so that you may be mature and complete, not lacking anything.

JAMES 1:2-4

HOPE IS ALWAYS STRONGER than you think. Trust it—and you will find the strength and courage you need.

For it is the very process of sharing hope—of loving each other, encouraging each other, building up each other, helping each other in practical ways—that produces more and more hope in all of us.

Peace does not dwell in outward things, but in the heart prepared to wait trustfully and quietly on him who has all things safely in his hands.

ELISABETH ELLIOT

Cast all your anxiety on him because he cares for you.

I PETER 5:7

[We have] a faith and knowledge resting on the hope of eternal life, which God, who does not lie, promised before the beginning of time.

TITUS 1:2

I HOPE I CAN REMEMBER his timing the next time I hear my teeth grinding because God is taking so long to answer my prayers, when I'm ready for results and the only answer I seem to get is "Not yet."

I will remember the deeds of the Lord; yes, I will remember your miracles of long ago. I will meditate on all your works and consider all your mighty deeds. Your ways, O God, are holy. What god is so great as our God? You are the God who performs miracles; you display your power among the peoples. With your mighty arm you redeemed your people.

PSALM 77:11-15

I HOPE I CAN REMEMBER to trust…because God knows the end from the beginning.

Hope and patience are two

sovereign remedies for all,

the surest reposals, the softest

cushions to lean on in adversity.

ROBERT BURTON

May the God of hope fill you with all joy and peace as you trust in him, so that you may overflow with hope by the power of the Holy Spirit.

ROMANS 15:13

forgive

I HOPE I CAN REMEMBER to keep on forgiving and asking forgiveness, even when I don't feel like doing it…because forgiveness is one of God's most useful tools for changing lives.

Be joyful always; pray continually; give thanks in all circumstances, for this is God's will for you in Christ Jesus.

1 THESSALONIANS 5:16-18

If anyone could tell you the shortest, surest way

to all happiness and perfection,

he must tell you to make it a rule to yourself

to thank and praise God for everything that happens to

you. For it is certain that whatever seeming calamity

happens to you, if you thank and praise God for it,

you turn it into a blessing.

WILLIAM LAW

In the battles most of us are facing, there are only two

options where being courageous is concerned—

and turning around and going back is not one of them.

We can choose to live through the days before us,

or we can choose not to live. Choosing not to live is

cowardly…No matter what it is that brings you to a

difficult place—death, illness, divorce, or even betrayal—

God intends for you to leave it with new life.

And it is not your own strength that will bring it forth.

SANDY CLOUGH

I HAVE NO DOUBTS that God would have supported and sustained me even if I had only come to know him after the first big rains began in my life. It is a mark of his grace that it is never too late to come to him.

I am still confident of this:
I will see the goodness of
the Lord in the land of the
living. Wait for the Lord; be
strong and take heart and
wait for the Lord.

PSALM 27:13-14

NO MATTER WHERE I GO, no matter what happens, my
God is always with me—suffering alongside me,
working to redeem my pain, sustaining and
supporting me in my weakness, shaping me into
the person he wants me to be.

God is always there.

I always knew it.

But now I *know* it.

And in your own time of testing, if you keep yourself
open to his working in your life, I know you will
know it, too.

But he said to me, "My grace is sufficient for you, for my power is made perfect in weakness." Therefore I will boast all the more gladly about my weaknesses, so that Christ's power may rest on me. That is why, for Christ's sake, I delight in…difficulties. For when I am weak, then I am strong.

2 CORINTHIANS 12:9-10

thankful

I HOPE I REMEMBER to thank him today for what will happen tomorrow…because thankfulness keeps my heart hopeful and open to receiving his blessings.

To find true hope, you have to go the distance between the head and the heart.

But as for me, I will always have hope; I will
praise you more and more. My mouth will tell
of your righteousness, of your salvation all day
long, though I know not its measure…
Your righteousness reaches to the skies,
O God, you who have done great things.
Who, O God, is like you? Though you have
made me see troubles, many and bitter,
you will restore my life again; from the depths
of the earth you will again bring me up. You will
increase my honor and comfort me once again.

PSALM 71:14-15, 19-21

AT THE VERY SAME MOMENT that life seems darkest, the sun is dancing beautifully off those puffy, inviting clouds.

No matter how thick the clouds and how hard the rain, you see, the sun is still shining.

Never lose an opportunity of seeing anything
that is beautiful; for beauty is God's handwriting—
a wayside sacrament. Welcome it in every fair face,
in every fair sky, in every flower,
and thank God for it as a cup of blessing.

RALPH WALDO EMERSON

Let us hold unswervingly to
the hope we profess, for he
who promised is faithful.

HEBREWS 10:23

MOST IMPORTANT, our Lord and Savior Jesus Christ has promised that the sunshine is the place we belong—and the sun is always shining.

It's the sunshine that never ends.

Now faith is being sure of
what we hope for and certain
of what we do not see.
This is what the ancients
were commended for.

HEBREWS 11:1-2

May our Lord Jesus Christ
himself and God our Father,
who loved us and by his
grace gave us eternal
encouragement and good
hope, encourage your hearts
and strengthen you in every
good deed and word.

2 THESSALONIANS 2:16-17